What's in this book

This book belongs to

_____

你见过它吗?
Have you ever seen it?

学习内容 Contents

沟通 Communication

描述动物外貌
Describe animals

生词 New words

★ 它	it
★ 鱼	fish
★ 鸟	bird
★ 有	to have
★ 没有	not to have
★ 长	long
★ 大	big
身体	body
翅膀	wing

句式 Sentence patterns

它有翅膀。
It has wings.

它有长长的身体。
It has a long body.

它没有耳朵。
It does not have ears.

跨学科学习 Project

认识动物的行动方式
Learn about how animals move

文化 Cultures

中西文化中的凤凰
The phoenix in Chinese and Western cultures

Get ready

1 What is the biggest fish in the world?

2 What is the biggest bird in the world?

3 What is the strangest animal in your mind?

tā
它

niǎo
鸟

yú
鱼

它是鱼，也是鸟。

cháng

长

它有长长的身体。

dà
大

它有大大的翅膀。

你见过它吗？

没有人见过它，因为……

它生活在神话里。

Let's think

1 Look at the pictures and think. Put a tick or a cross.

这是鸟。 ☐

这是鸟。 ☐

这是鱼。 ☐

这是鱼。 ☐

2 Draw your favourite animal and talk about it.

New words

1 Learn the new words.

鸟

翅膀

长

它

鱼

身体

没有

有

大

2 Circle the correct pictures.

有 没有 长长的鱼 大大的鸟

听听说说 Listen and say

03 **1** Listen and guess. Write the letters.

04 **2** Look at the pictures. Listen to the sto

① 这是什么?

② 它有大大的嘴巴和身体。

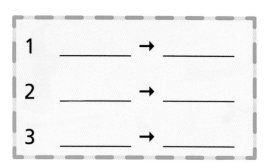

1 _____ → _____

2 _____ → _____

3 _____ → _____

这是鸭嘴兽，platypus。
你见过它吗？

它有没有翅膀？

它没有翅膀。

3 Listen to your teacher and guess. Write the letters.

它有大大的耳朵和身体，
它有长长的鼻子，
它喜欢吃香蕉，
它是什么？

a

b

c

d

它没有翅膀，
它喜欢玩，
它喜欢吃鱼，
它是什么？

它有长长的身体，
它没有翅膀，
没有人见过它，
它是什么？

Task

Show a photo of your favourite animal and introduce it to your friends.

我喜欢熊猫 (panda)。
它有大大的身体。
它没有翅膀。

Paste your photo here.

Game

Count in Chinese to check if the numbers of fish and birds in the pictures are correct.

29

21

Song

 **Listen and sing.**

它是鱼，

它是长长的鱼。

它是鸟，

它是大大的鸟。

长长的鱼，你见过吗？

大大的鸟，你见过吗？

课堂用语 Classroom language

翻开书本第8页。

Turn to page 8.

打开书包。

Open the school bag.

写一写 Write

1 Learn and trace the stroke.

横撇

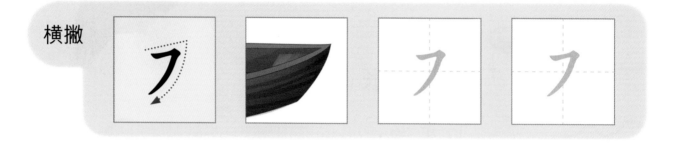

2 Learn the component. Circle 鱼 in the characters.

鱼　鲸　鲨　鱼　鲜

3 The writing of 鱼 has changed over time. Look at the characters and colour the fish.

4 Trace and write the character.

ノ　ク　夕　ク　夕　角　角　鱼

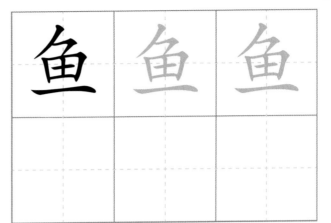

汉字小常识 Did you know?

Can you match the pictures to the scripts? Write the letters.

Ancient scripts are generally pictures of things. About 600 of them are still in use today.

a 羊　　b 马　　c 鸟　　d 虎　　e 牛

Cultures

1 The phoenix is an ancient mythical creature in both the East and the West. Have you ever seen one?

In China, phoenix is an important symbol of peace, nobility and beauty.

In the West, phoenix is associated with the sun and rebirth, symbolizing renewal.

2 Colour the phoenix and talk about it.

它有大大的翅膀。

它……

Project

1 Group the animals by how they move. Write the numbers.

Fly
_____

Swim
_____

Walk
_____

2 Can you find any animal which can both fly and swim? Show and describe it.

它的……

它有……

它是……

19

 Checkpoint

1 Answer the questions from Sphinx to get into the pyramid.

Can you write the character 'fish'?

它喜欢吃什么？

它有没有翅膀？

Can you say 'It has a big mouth' in Chinese?

Can you say 'It has a big body' in Chinese?

你见过我吗？

它是什么？

你几岁？

我叫 Sphinx。你叫什么名字？

2 Work with your friend. Colour the stars and the chillies.

Words and sentences	说	读	写
它	☆	☆	🌶
鱼	☆	☆	☆
鸟	☆	☆	🌶
有	☆	☆	🌶
没有	☆	☆	🌶
长	☆	☆	🌶
大	☆	☆	🌶
身体	☆	🌶	🌶
翅膀	☆	🌶	🌶
它有翅膀。	☆	🌶	🌶
它有长长的身体。	☆	🌶	🌶
它没有耳朵。	☆	🌶	🌶

Describe animals	☆

3 What does your teacher say?

分享 Sharing

Words I remember

它	tā	it
鱼	yú	fish
鸟	niǎo	bird
有	yǒu	to have
没有	méi yǒu	not to have
长	cháng	long
大	dà	big
身体	shēn tǐ	body
翅膀	chì bǎng	wing

Other words

也	yě	also, too
人	rén	people, person
见过	jiàn guo	to have seen
吗	ma	(question word)
因为	yīn wèi	because
生活	shēng huó	to live
在	zài	at, in
神话	shén huà	myth
里	lǐ	inside
鸭嘴兽	yā zuǐ shòu	platypus
熊猫	xióng māo	panda

OXFORD

UNIVERSITY PRESS

Oxford University Press is a department of the University of Oxford.
It furthers the University's objective of excellence in research, scholarship,
and education by publishing worldwide. Oxford is a registered trade mark of
Oxford University Press in the UK and in certain other countries

Published in Hong Kong by
Oxford University Press (China) Limited
39th Floor, One Kowloon, 1 Wang Yuen Street, Kowloon Bay,
Hong Kong

Illustrated by Anne Lee, KK Ng, KY Chan and Wildman

Photographs for reproduction permitted by Dreamstime.com

China National Publications Import & Export (Group) Corporation is an authorized distributor of
Oxford Elementary Chinese.

Please contact content@cnpiec.com.cn or 86-10-65856782

ISBN: 978-0-19-082143-2

10 9 8 7 6 5 4 3 2